ICING ON THE CAKE

په کیک باندې ملائ

English Food Idioms

(Pashto - English)

د خوراکونو په اړه انګلیسي محاورې

(پښتو- انګلیسي)

By Troon Harrison

Illustrated by Joyeeta Neogi

Pashto translation by Tariq Kamal

Language Lizard

Basking Ridge

For English audio and resources for teaching idioms, see the last page of this book.

Icing on the Cake - English Food Idioms (Pashto-English)

Published by Language Lizard
Basking Ridge, NJ 07920
info@LanguageLizard.com

Visit us at www.LanguageLizard.com

LCCN: 2020905419 (English)

ISBN: 978-1-63685-516-5 (Print)

WHAT IS AN IDIOM?

An idiom is a phrase that says one thing but means something different. An idiom can be a quick way of saying something complicated. Knowing idioms will help you to understand and speak English fluently. This book contains idioms about food.

*Note - The English idioms are translated **literally**.*

محاوره څه ته وائي؟

محاوره هغه جملي ته وئيلي شي كومه چې په وينه کي يو شان وي ولي مطلب ئي بل څه وي. كيدي شي يوه محاوره د يو ګراني خبري كولو آسانه لار وي. د محاورو پيژندل به تاسو سره مرسته وكړي چې په انګليسي ژبه پوه شئ او خبرې وكړئ. دا كتاب د خوراكونو په اړه محاورې لري.

يادونه - دا انګليسي محاورې په **لفظي** توګه ژباړل شوي.

SELLING LIKE HOT CAKES

د ګرمو کیکونو په څیر خرڅول

Meaning: Something is selling very fast

معني: کله چي یو څیز ډیر زر زر خرسیګي

The fresh, ripe melons were so delicious they were **selling like hot cakes**.

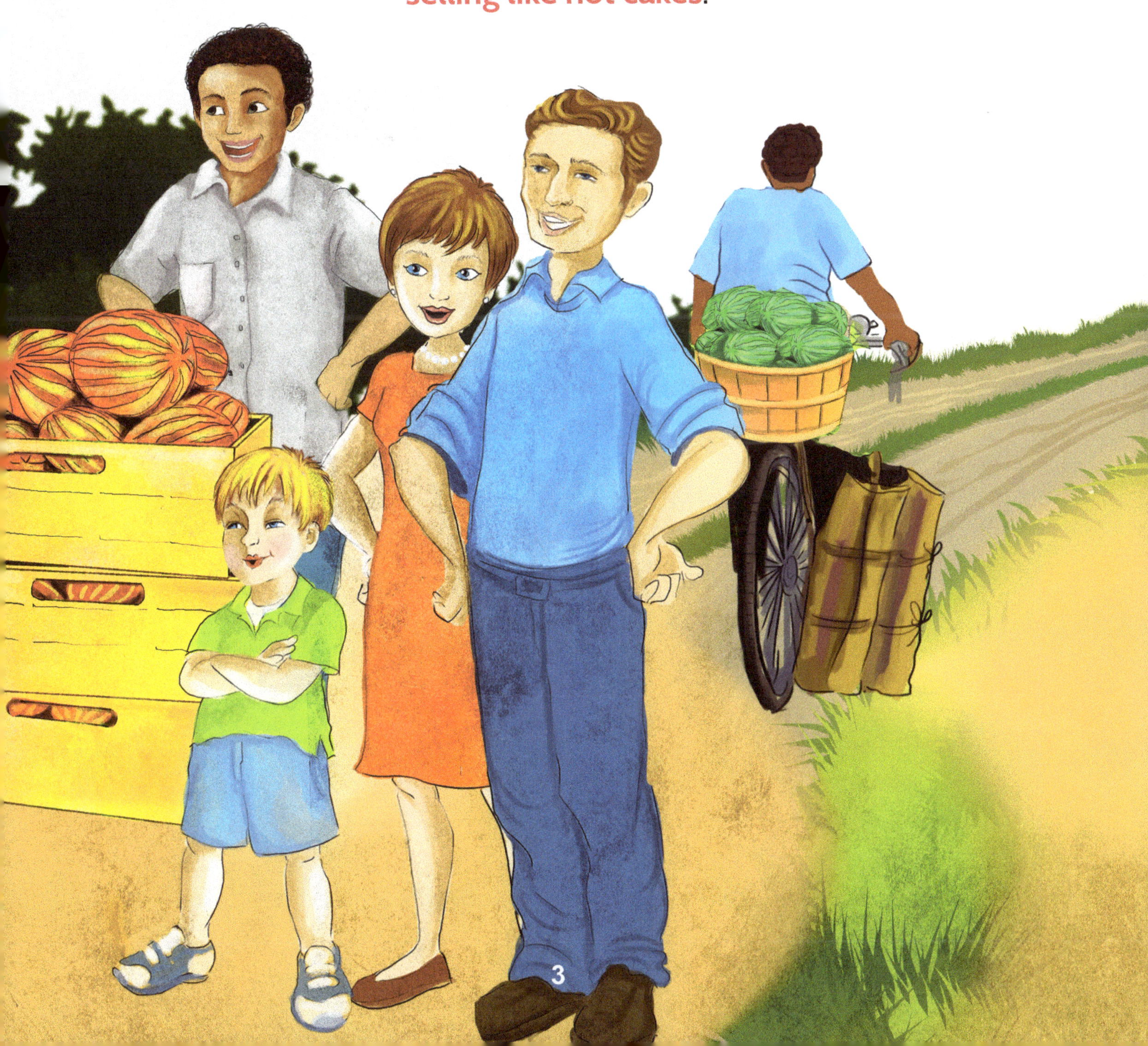

A COUCH POTATO

د صوفې آلو

Meaning: A person spends hours watching TV or relaxing

معنی: هغه بنده چې ډیر وختتلویزیون ګوري یا آرام کوي

She worked hard all week, but on weekends she was a couch potato.

BIGGER FISH TO FRY

د پخولو لپاره لوی کب

Meaning: Doing something that is more important

معني: هغه څه کول چې ډېر مهم وي

I wanted my brother to come sailing with me, but he had **bigger fish to fry.**

USE YOUR NOODLE
د خپل نوډل نه کار واخلئ

Meaning: Use your brain to figure out something for yourself

معني: د ځان لپاره يو څه معلومولو لپاره د خپل دماغ څخه کار اخيستل

I wanted help tying my shoes, but Dad told me to use my noodle.

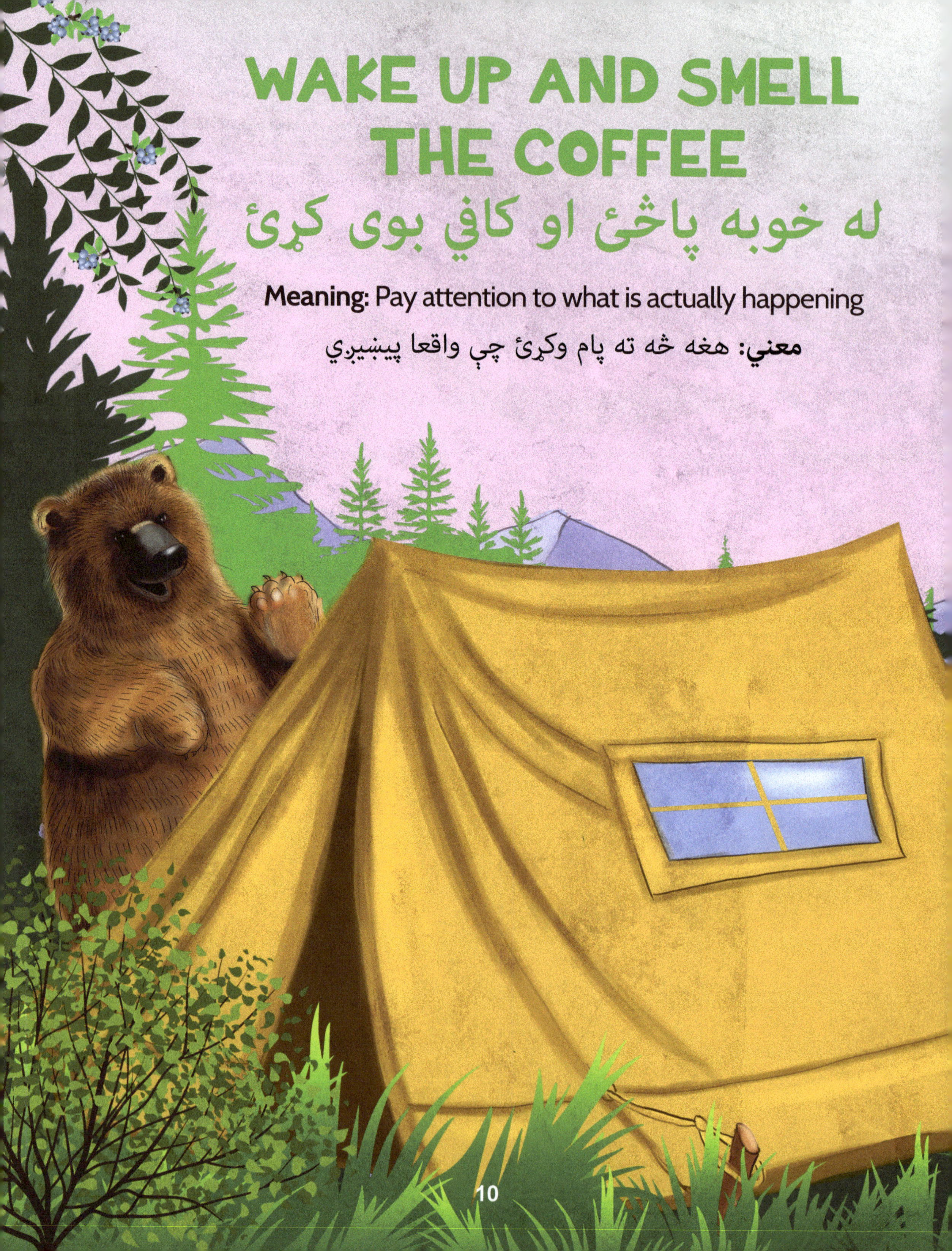

WAKE UP AND SMELL THE COFFEE

له خوبه پاڅئ او کافي بوی کړئ

Meaning: Pay attention to what is actually happening

معني: هغه څه ته پام وکړئ چې واقعا پیښیږي

The cowboy thought it was a safe place to camp, but he needed to **wake up and smell the coffee**.

SPILL THE BEANS

لوبیا توی کړئ

Meaning: To confess and reveal a secret

معني: د یو راز اعتراف او ښکاره کول

When the stray puppy howled, the children had to spill the beans.

CRY OVER SPILLED MILK

په توى شوي شاودو ژړل

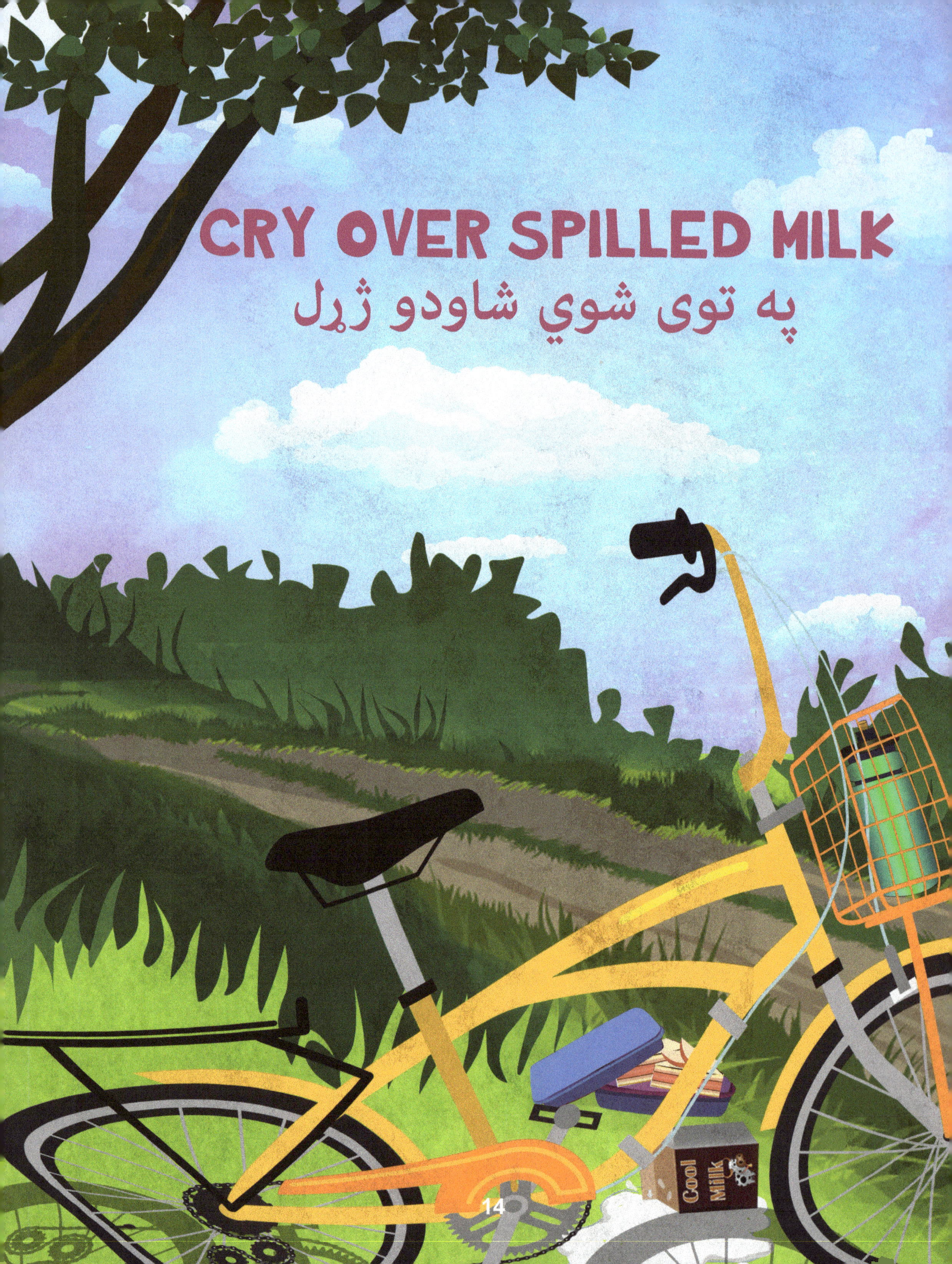

Meaning: To be upset about something that cannot be changed

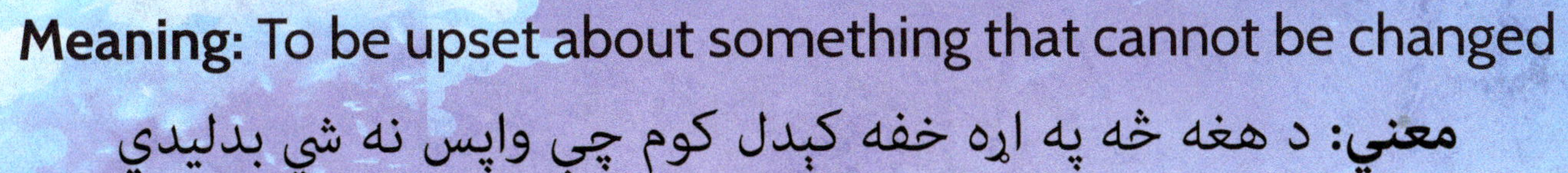
معني: د هغه څه په اړه خفه کېدل کوم چې واپس نه شي بدليدي

I was upset about my bike, but Mom told me not to cry over spilled milk.

APPLE OF MY EYE

زما د سترګو منړا

Meaning: Something a person loves very much

معني: هغه څه چې انسان ورسره ډېره مينه کوي

After my camel won the race, he was the apple of my eye.

GOING BANANAS
کیلا کیدل

Meaning: Acting crazy

معني: د لیونو پشان حرکات کول

The boy I was watching was going bananas.

23
32

TWO PEAS IN A POD
په یو کنډول کې دوه مټر

Meaning: Two people who are very similar

معني: دوه کسان چې ډېر یو بل پشان وي

My children always play together, like **two peas in a pod**.

WITH A GRAIN OF SALT

د مالګې د دانې سره

Meaning: To be skeptical

معني: شکمن کېدل

My hairdresser said my new hairstyle suited me, but I took her words **with a grain of salt**.

PIE IN THE SKY
په اسمان کي انعام

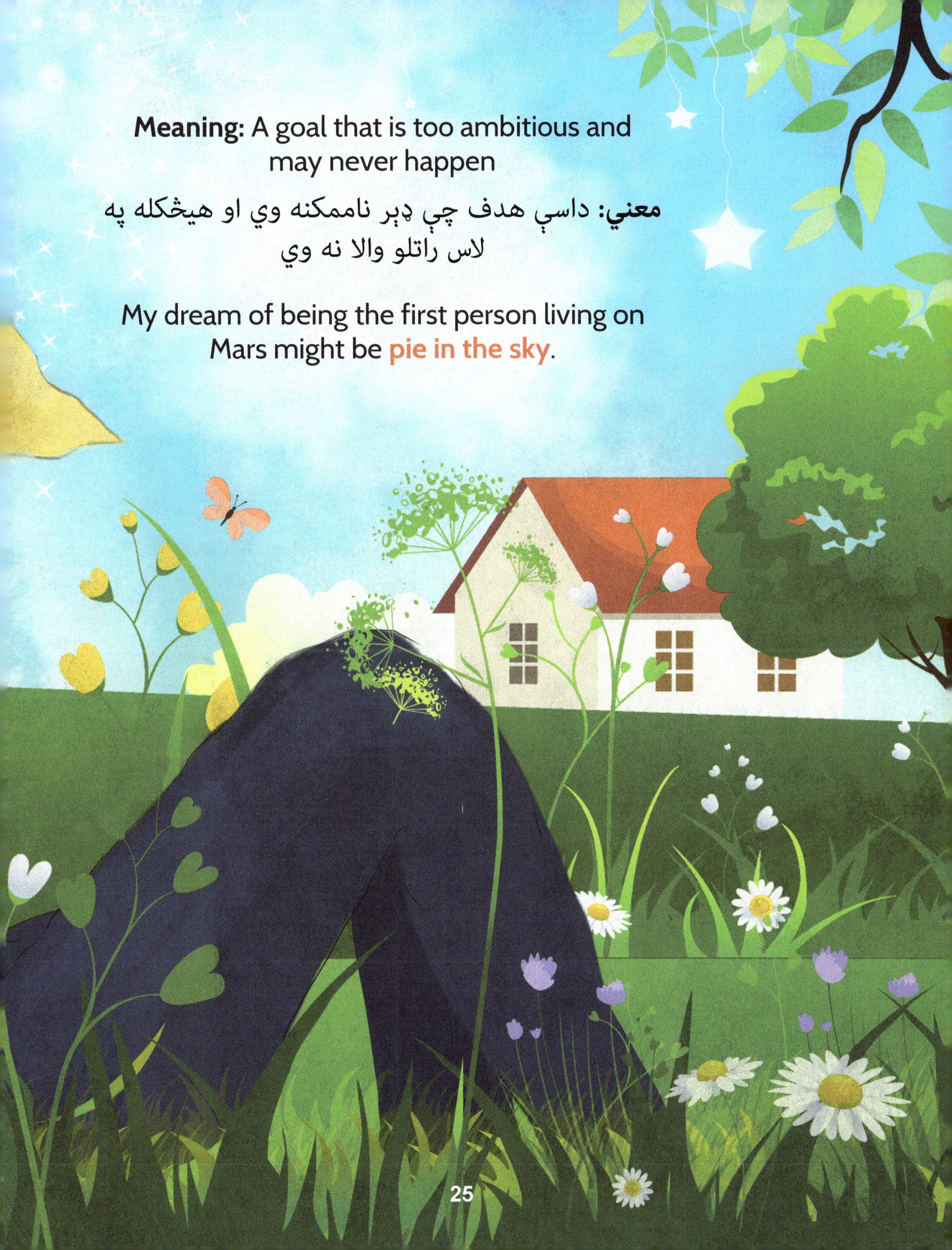

Meaning: A goal that is too ambitious and may never happen

معني: داسې هدف چې ډېر ناممکنه وي او هیڅکله په لاس راتلو والا نه وي

My dream of being the first person living on Mars might be pie in the sky.

THE BIG CHEESE

لوی پیراوي

Meaning: A person who is important and powerful

معني: هغه څوک چې مهم او ځواکمن وي

The farmer owned so many goats, she thought she was **the big cheese**.

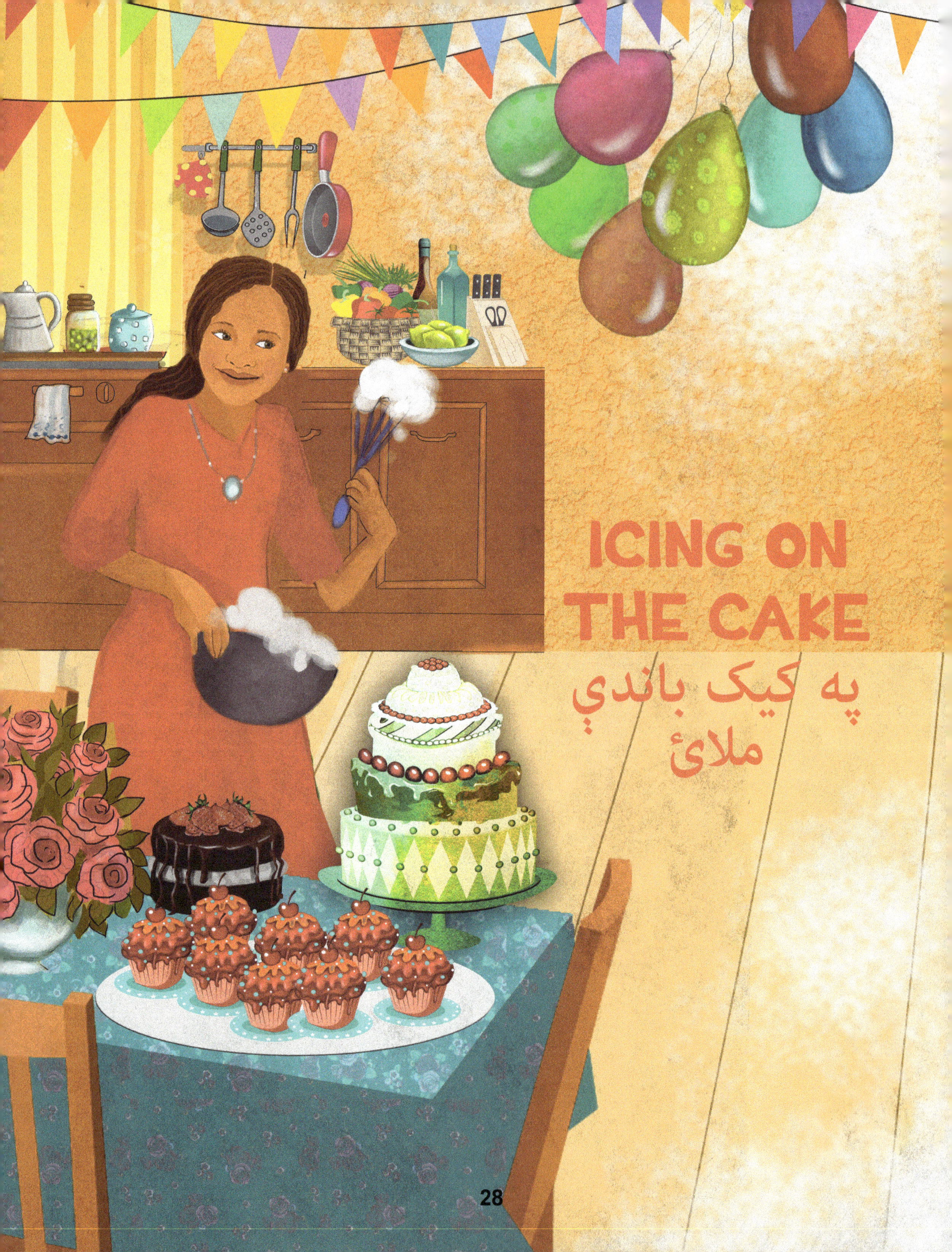

ICING ON THE CAKE

په کیک باندې
ملائ

Meaning: Something which is an extra special treat

معني: چا سره د ضرورت نه سیوا ډیر ښه سلوک کول

My grandfather's surprise visit was the icing on the cake.

Visit www.LanguageLizard.com/Food-Idioms for additional resources for teaching and learning English idioms, including:

- English audio of this book
- Multicultural lesson plans for use in the classroom or at home
- Information on the origin of the idioms in this book
- Additional food idioms with their meaning, usage, and origin
- Information on idiom translations and idioms in other languages

This book is part of the **Language Lizard Idiom Series**.

Visit **www.LanguageLizard.com** for a complete listing of the titles in this series and available languages.

www.ingramcontent.com/pod-product-compliance
Lightning Source LLC
LaVergne TN
LVHW071725230826
846093LV00024B/534
* 9 7 8 1 6 3 6 8 5 5 1 6 5 *